GW01072091

WHO IS
FATHER CHRISTMAS?

Shirley Harrison

DAVID & CHARLES
Newton Abbot   London   North Pomfret (Vt)

(*Opposite page*) Phoning Santa Claus by Thomas Nast.
Mary Evans Picture Library

I would particularly like to thank Jean Maulden, Tunbridge
Wells Reference Library; Çağlar Yasal, Turkish Tourist Office;
Jim Hawkins, UK Press Officer for New York State; Camilla
Gior, Royal Norwegian Embassy; Phyllis Chapman, Finnish
Tourist Board; Aliki Fanos, National Tourist Organisation of
Greece; Intourist; and my mother—who replaced my stocking
with a pillowcase.

British Library Cataloguing in Publication Data

Harrison, Shirley
    Who is Father Christmas?
    1. Santa Claus
    I. Title
    398'.352   GT4985

    ISBN 0-7153-8222-5

Text and original illustrations © Shirley Harrison 1981

Typeset by ABM Typographics Limited, Hull
and printed in Great Britain
by Biddles Limited, Guildford, Surrey
for David & Charles (Publishers) Limited
Brunel House   Newton Abbot   Devon

Published in the United States of America
by David & Charles Inc
North Pomfret   Vermont 05053   USA

CONTENTS

JOLLY OLD CHRISTMAS.

Jolly Old Christmas from *The Illustrated London News*, 1844. *Mary Evans Picture Library*

QUESTIONS

Father Christmas is alive and well and living in Greenland . . .
Lapland . . . the North Pole . . . who can say? Letters sent to
Father Christmas c/o almost anywhere are sure of a personal
reply. He has survived wars, persecution and religious upheaval,
because for centuries grown-ups have loved and cherished him
in one form or another. Only 100 years ago were children too
allowed to share their parents' fantasies and began to hang
hopeful stockings out.

Electric lights have banished many of the countryside's dark
corners, on which imagination used to feed; but they have not
defeated the mysterious midnight visitor who cheers the
wintry evenings now in so many parts of the world.

We pretend that the stockings, the trees and the reindeer
belong only to childhood; that we grown-ups play the game of
Christmas make-believe 'just for the sake of the children'. But
it is not like that at all.

After all, it is not the children who invite Father Christmas
to the office party; nor is it children who are photographed on
his knee in the smart ski resorts of France; or hire red fur-
trimmed outfits for their dogs in New York, or shake his hand
outside the Church of the Nativity in Bethlehem!

It is so easy for Europeans to wonder at the current American
slick, professional treatment of a beloved institution. But it was
the Americans in the first place who absorbed the ancient
traditions of many new European immigrants, shook them
all together and produced the Father Christmas–Santa Claus
cocktail, which in Victorian hands became a rather sweet and
sickly mix. It was the Americans not so long ago who, with
their usual energetic enthusiasm, gave the jolly ho-hoing Walt
Disney character to the world. They dressed him in Father

Christmas clothes and they called him Santa Claus. With typical showmanship they built him fairy grottoes guarded by plastic reindeer; and we all took him to our hearts.

Now, despite the commercial overkill, that 'Santa-Christmas' figure is busier than ever before. Yet what do we know of him? Who is he? Who were his ancestors? Where does he come from? Why does he visit us at all? He may not be today what we imagine he *ought* to be . . . but can we be sure? Father Christmas and Santa Claus may look alike but are they really related?

Once we begin to probe their origins we find that that bulging sack is full of surprises, but unwrapping the facts does not need to spoil the fun. If we understand the genealogy of our own legend we can get on with the fun and games surrounding his modern earthly impersonators. They are, after all, just a mirror of their brash, supermarket times much as the Roman King of Saturnalia or the Tudor Lord of Misrule were of theirs before them. The spirit of Father Christmas himself is immortal and international.

Winter walking the streets. *Courtesy of Weidenfeld & Nicolson*

THE PAGAN BEGINNINGS

The love of ritual folklore is one which all men share. Very often, tribes thousands of miles apart, in climates as varied as the Arctic or the American desert, have told the same tales generation after generation around their camp fires of an evening, with the same symbolism and strikingly similar heroes and villains. These stories were often adopted and adapted centuries ago by more civilised cultures and religions and passed down to us, whose deep-seated need for simple make-believe is as great as it has ever been.

Our own Father Christmas really began his long journey through the night across the dark skies of pre-history and long before the appearance of 'Santa Claus', and his ancestral roots can be traced far and wide.

Wherever the winters were long and gloomy men devised mid-season festivals to cheer themselves and herald the coming spring. The granaries were still full and the annual slaughter of stock was over, so the time was ripe for feasting. But there was, too, a religious motivation – a wish to placate the forces of darkness and to honour the gods who would, hopefully, restore the sun and with it the fertility of the countryside.

These festivals were frequently ribald, gluttonous affairs lasting for days and often made special by the visit of some fearsome god-like being, or spirits who were said to appear from the wintry nights to punish or reward. Originally these beings did not bring gifts – they were purely the creation of grown-ups to feed the grown-up imagination in a dark world lit only by the eerie magic of the moon, and the children shared their elders' awe.

At the time of the birth of Christ, to the peoples of the north, Odin, 'the Allfather' was the greatest and wisest of the Gods and was worshipped in Britain too, as Woden. His wife was Frigga and his son was Thor, God of Thunder. For centuries, the black-bearded Odin flashed through the skies of northern Europe in his chariot of molten gold, drawn by his horses Early Waker and Allstrong. To Christians in some places he became synonymous with the Devil – not surprising because wherever he went his ravens Hugin and Mugin were perched upon his shoulders. With his sacred spear, Gungnir, his blue cloak flying and his gleaming gold winged helmet, he was a mighty figure. Occasionally, though, in his search for wisdom Odin wandered the world disguised. When on his earthly travels he rode the famous huge eight-legged white horse, Sleipir, and sometimes wore a coolie-style hat to hide the fact that he was blind in one eye.

Men believed that Odin lived in Valhalla, his palace in the sky where the souls of dead heroes were welcomed. Valhalla – or Heaven – was situated just above the World Tree – Yggdrasil – which linked Heaven with Hell and upon which Odin once hung himself for forty days to learn something of eternal truth.

Across most of the north, Yule (the Scandinavian word for pre-Christian midwinter festivities) was the season when the ghosts of Valhalla were released to roam the countryside looking for evil-doers. Odin himself was then thought to lead a terrible, demonic hunt – known in Britain later as Herlathing – which swept howling through the wintry nights in a roar of wind, carrying off naughty children.

Long after Europe became totally Christian, people used to leave out grain to feed Sleipir and food to appease the spirits. In many rural places as the memory of Odin faded, there were other things to go bump in the night and preoccupy the peasant. Germany evolved the grisly Knecht Ruprecht with his long,

red tongue and flashing eyes. In Greece the hideous Kallikantzaroi terrorised villagers. The Kallikantzaroi were rather worse
than the licentious centaurs of ancient mythology – they were
half man, half beast; black and hairy with long curved nails,
monkeys' arms, bloody tongues, tusks and either asses's ears
or goats' horns. During the twelve days around Christmas they
ran amok – and people feared that unless they had their homes
purified by a priest or left food as a peace offering in the
chimney the Kallikantzaroi would destroy everything.

Even now all these legends linger – and we perform the same
rituals, though our Christmas visitors are gentle, kindly bene-
factors. So children put out corn or milk or even mince pies for
the friendly reindeer, or for Santa's horse in Holland, the Wise
Men's camels in Spain or the busy Christmas goblins in
Iceland.

SATURN

For Romans in the Southern Latin lands in the year of Christ's
birth the notorious winter festivities of Saturnalia began around
14 December and ended on 24 December, to be followed on 25
December by Juvenilia (the Feast of the Children which became
the mediaeval Christian Feast of Innocents). In January there
was the important Feast of Kalends.

The Roman God of Peace and Plenty who ruled over the
revels was Saturn (sometimes known as Cronos the Charioteer)
and his feast recalled a Golden Age when all men were equal
and all were happy. The celebrations were marked, according
to the poet Lucian, by 'drinking and being drunk, noise and
games and dice, appointing of Kings and feasting of slaves,
singing naked, clapping of tremulous hands and an occasional
ducking of corked faces in icy water'.

Certainly during Saturnalia the established order was turned
topsy turvy. Men dressed as women, slaves were freed and
dressed as their masters. In the armed forces today there is the
same delight at upsetting the established order – the officers

Odin

wait on the ranks at Christmas dinner! In many places clay or paste images were made to be sold as presents at the street fairs – just as in modern Rome the Piazza Navona is handed over at Christmas to hundreds of stall-holders selling paste and clay cribs and Christian figurines. Apart from that, says Lucian 'all business, be it public or private, is forbidden during feast days . . . let none follow their avocations saving cooks and bakers'.

To keep an earthly eye on the frolics a 'king' was elected, usually from the army – originally to represent Saturn, but he became no more than an early version of the mediaeval Lord of Misrule, a Roman 'MC'. He was allowed to make his own laws for the period of the holiday and to enforce any ridiculous whims he might entertain, such as ordering his guests to strip.

In his original exalted position he was rather like our Father Christmas – a stand-in for the real thing. But there was one very important difference. The reward for the honour was a glorious – but compulsory – suicide when it was all over!

There was no similar figurehead presiding over the Festival of Kalends which followed, though Kalends itself, being the time for election of consuls, was a far more important holiday and was enjoyed throughout the Roman Empire. It is quite likely that the Holy St Nicholas, who eventually became 'Santa Claus', himself watched the frolics in fourth-century Asia Minor where he was Bishop, for certainly many Christians joined in, much as many Jewish people today send Christmas cards and have a turkey.

Like Saturnalia, Kalends was an extravaganza of too much food, drink and debauchery. It was a time to decorate the houses with greenery and special lighting effects and most of all to give presents – especially to children. (These little gifts were known as *strenae*, a word which survives in the French word for New Year present – *etrennes*.) Most of all it was the time when revellers dressed in animal skins and grotesque, demonic masks – a custom which played an important part in mediaeval

11

Saturnalia

drama and mummers' plays. All that remains for us today is the Christmas paper hat.

Libanius, a Greek writer in the fourth century, noted 'He who the whole year has taken pleasure in saving and piling up his pennies becomes suddenly extravagant . . . a stream of presents pours itself out on all sides.' Plus ça change!

THE SHAMAN

Meanwhile in the faraway wastelands of the Arctic, in Siberia, Northern Canada and Greenland and amongst the Indian tribes which wandered the undiscovered American continent, there was another little-known mysterious midwinter visitor who descended from the sky to bring rewards and punishments.

The shaman was – and is today – a hybrid priest, medicine man, witch doctor whose mystical powers were invoked to ensure the spiritual welfare of the tribe. Because in many of these places the reindeer was a vital part of tribal life, it too assumed a religious importance.

The shaman could travel between the three realms of Heaven, Earth and Hell by inducing an ecstatic trance and so was able to intercede with the gods or the devils. It is known that these flights of fancy could be produced by eating the hallucinogenic mushroom, Fly Agaric – a favourite snack for the reindeer too!

So there was the shaman – alias Odin – alias Saturn – alias Father Christmas, flying with his reindeer through the skies . . . a pre-Christian junkie!

What is more, these tribes – widespread as they were – each erected a shaman stick through the smokehole during the midwinter feast. This shaman stick symbolised the transcendental path through the three cosmic levels.

In simple terms it seems very like our Father Christmas coming down the chimney, into the igloo, tepee, or underground hovel. And what was the shaman stick, Yggdrazil or the Old Testament Tree of Knowledge, has now become the Christmas tree, no longer topped by a Norse bird, messenger from Heaven, but by a fairy or an angel. The symbols have changed, but the meaning and the magic have remained.

So, in the year that Jesus was born Odin, Saturn and the shaman were watching over their respective parts of the world. In the hot and dusty culture of His birthplace in Judea, Jews themselves celebrated the midwinter Festival of Hanukkah, with gift giving.

Early Christians saw no reason to mark the birth of Christ, especially since the exact date was not even recorded. They preferred to honour His baptism fixed on 6 January and known later as Epiphany. But eventually this was not enough. Christ-

13

Shaman

ianity needed a midwinter feast of its own, to counteract the degenerate pagan razzmatazz with which it was surrounded.

In about AD 350 Pope Julius I settled judiciously on the Roman Soltis – the Dies Natalis Invicti. This was the day on which followers of Mithras – the most serious rival to Christ – had already fixed their curiously Christian-sounding 'Birthday of the Unconquered Sun'. In many places the birth of Mithras was already marked by processions in which the statue of a virgin was carried, holding a tiny baby.

In choosing this date as the birthday of the Christian Son of God, Julius offered an alternative reason for celebration. Even so, the word Christmas was not recorded in England until 1034 when it appears in the Anglo-Saxon Chronicle instead of the usual 'Midwinter Mass'.

Gradually Christianity absorbed many of the pagan symbols and adapted them; the holly, which was once symbolic of Moses' burning bush and was popular in Roman house decoration as a winter evergreen, was later identified with Jesus' crown of thorns and believed to protect against witches. The druids' Golden Bough – mistletoe – with its magical powers of healing and fertility was frowned on by the Church, however.

As the threads were woven together through the centuries and the old ways faded into history, in many places Christians themselves dreamed up a host of phantom figures to replace the old Gods or to create their own neighbourhood spirits. Among them, in Britain, was Father Christmas. He was no God, nor was he worshipped and he was not even very important.

Father Christmas showed his pagan origins, representing the temporal, rumbustious side of Christmas and reflecting man's fundamental need for an occasional fling. He crops up first in mediaeval drama as a bearded but rather ill-defined 'presenter', but he is clearly a descendant of Odin, distantly related perhaps to Saturn.

Elsewhere the real life Bishop Nicholas of Myra had already become, *vox populi*, a saint. He was never canonised by the Church but was adopted by the faithful throughout the continent and became the busiest, most popular of them all. His role as a good man was originally deeply religious and not connected with children, but in time his ecclesiastical halo dimmed a little and he, too, became a folk hero.

From about the twelfth century the unholy 'Father Christmas' and the Holy Santa Nicholas were to begin a remote if friendly rivalry which has finally come to a head in this century.

SAINT NICHOLAS

In 1969 under the revisionary eye of Pope Paul VI the gentle St Nicholas was ignominiously removed from the Roman Catholic calendar of saints. His feast day – 6 December –

became just another day. The Church was no longer convinced that his miracles and many acts of piety were any more than old wives' tales and so, after 1500 years, he was officially relegated to the ranks of Woden and old Father Christmas himself in the shadowy border land between legend and history.

Sad, because Nicholas was real enough and his following had been greater than for almost any other saint. In England alone during the Middle Ages over 400 churches had been dedicated to him. Throughout Europe he had become a symbol for kindly generosity, especially to children, and the inspiration for harmless merrymaking every St Nicholas' Eve. Fortunately his demotion made no difference to his popularity.

Nicholas was born in Patara in Turkey around the year AD 270. Legend says that from the beginning his holiness was remarkable.On the day of his birth he stood up and joined his hands in prayerful thanksgiving. On fast days he even refused his mother's breast.

When his parents died in an epidemic he gave away their fortune and became a priest. Such goodness stood him in good stead for he became Bishop of Myra, near the modern village of Demre, a thriving town on the Mediterranean coast which had been visited by St Paul on his way to Rome. There, during the reign of Diocletian, Nicholas was a tireless fighter for his Christian principles. He was probably martyred for them around AD 342.

There are very few historical records of Nicholas' life, but the stories multiplied after his death and he became something of a local folk hero. Not till 500 years later was he really 'discovered' and launched on the road to international fame – by another bishop, St Methodius of Constantinople, who wrote an imaginative and somewhat highly coloured biography of his fellow countryman. The book was the first documentary account of the saint's life which, polished and improved in the telling, formed the basis for the picture of St Nicholas which has been handed down to us.

It was St Methodosius' Nicholas who, through his unending

charity and generosity, became the patron saint and protector not only of children but of sailors, thieves and pawnbrokers. The three gold balls which hang outside today's pawnshop are believed to have originally represented the three bags of gold given to redeem the virtue of three maidens. They also became the symbol of the rich Medicis in fifteenth-century Italy and of the Lombards who were the first people to open pawnshops in Britain, in the thirteenth century.

Nicholas' reputation spread through the coastal towns of Europe until eventually he was adopted in Greece and Russia and – most important – by the city of Amsterdam, a decision that made sure of his claim to immortality. For it was the Dutch who were to turn him into a white-bearded Sinterklaas, resplendent in bishop's regalia, though his holy status was soon forgotten. It was the Dutch who took him with them when they colonised America, much later, in the seventeenth century, and founded the City of New Amsterdam – which was to become New York.

From St Methodosius' account it is not difficult to understand how the stories surrounding St Nicholas came about. He tells how three men were unjustly accused, tried and were about to be executed when St Nicholas appeared and persuaded the local governor to set them free. Some time later, he says, some Roman soldiers who were witnesses to the scene were themselves under sentence of death and prayed to St Nicholas for help. Sure enough, the saint appeared to the Emperor Constantine in a vision and he was persuaded to release them.

On another occasion, when famine threatened his people, St Nicholas travelled the countryside to comfort them. He stayed one night at an inn where he discovered the landlord had not only murdered three young boys but had pickled their bodies in brine and was planning to serve them up as a gastronomic treat for his guests. Miraculously, St Nicholas brought the children back to life and, to be on the safe side, converted the innkeeper.

Most famous of all the legends is that of St Nicholas and the three virgins and it is probably the one which gave rise to the story of Santa Claus. There was once a nobleman in Myra who had become so poor he could no longer afford a dowry for his three daughters. In desperation he had decided to offer them for prostitution. St Nicholas heard of the girls' plight and on three successive nights he crept secretly to their window and, unseen, threw in a bag of gold. One of these landed in a slipper, set by the fire to warm.

So the idea of the saint as a kindly bearer of gifts arose, distributing goodies in the dead of night, and centuries later children were encouraged to hang up a symbolic stocking or a shoe on St Nicholas' Eve in the hope he would not forget them.

But long before the legends of his gift-bringing role, the real St Nicholas was revered locally as a good man in the strictly religious sense. When he died, his remains were interred in the cathedral of ancient Myra and later transferred to the eighth-century Byzantine church in the village of Demre. There they were honoured until their safety was threatened by wars between Muslim and Christian. In 1087 some Italian sailors took the law into their own hands and raided the tomb of St Nicholas hoping to whisk the body away to safety in their own country.

According to the Italians the body now rests in Bari, on the heel of Italy, where an ornate basilica was built for it which became a centre of pilgrimage for Christians from all over Europe. According to the Turks it was not quite like that. In the scuffle at the tomb some of the tug-of-war relics were dropped and only part of St Nicholas reached Bari. The rest, including his jawbone and teeth, reposes in a museum showcase in Antalya, watched over by a somewhat irreverant cartoon Father Christmas poster, explaining how it all happened.

So, today's tourists, or pilgrims, may take their pick – Bari or Demre?

Visitors come to Bari all the year round to pray in the Basilica, for it is believed that a miraculous healing ointment –

St Nicholas from the fresco in the Church of St Nicholas, Demre

Mana di St Nicola – oozes still, from the silver-lined sar-cophagus containing the relics of the saint. Demoted or not, his religious spirit is as powerful and benevolent here as it has ever been.

In Bari each year, during the week commencing 7 May they commemorate the sea-borne arrival of their saint 900 years before, with a lavish festival. Dressed in their best, thousands of people throng onto the ancient harbour front; the streets are garlanded with flowers and bright with the sound of music everywhere. The crowds are waiting for the arrival of the carnival procession and a replica of the ship which brought the saint, which carries the 'body' of Nicholas and is to be drawn through the town by a team of sailors, down to the Basilica for an open-air Mass. As night falls, a full-sized statue of the saint is carried to the quayside and on to the leading boat. As the bands play every craft in Bari sets sail into the Mediterranean where they anchor, while the crowds on shore wait spellbound for the start of a firework spectacular from the sea.

In Turkey, so far, the St Nicholas connection is fairly low key. Most visitors to Demre come now for the archaeological remains of ancient Myra – the fourth-century Lykian rock tombs, the Roman Theatre and the Granary of Hadrian.

The village of Demre itself is no longer on the coast and the same alluvial deposits which have pushed back the sea also swallowed St Nicholas' church. Over the centuries it was damaged and repaired many times, then finally abandoned, until in the 1860s the Russians took an interest in the burial place of their patron. They spent a great deal of money on restoration but not until the last few years has the surrounding mud been removed – by the Turks themselves – to reveal some hitherto unknown parts of a very beautiful domed church rich in frescoes and mosaics, and the saint's vandalised tomb.

The Christian church in Demre is no longer alive but as tourists, having 'done' Greece, push eastwards it is ready to once more takes its place, along with Ephesus, the Virgin Mary's house and other Christian places of pilgrimage around the coast.

Most ironic of all – Muslim children in Turkey celebrate a special day on 1 January, when a red-coated, fur-trimmed 'Noel Baba' arrives to bring them presents in the dead of night. He wears a hood, not a bishop's mitre, so whether he is the cousin of our jolly northern Father Christmas or of their own compatriot, the saintly Nicholas, who can say?

THE JOURNEY
THROUGH TIME

Christmas festivities during the Middle Ages in Britain were a monument of excessive wining and dining and as spiritually intense and colourful as were the cathedral stained-glass windows. The Twelve Days of Christmas were a national holiday during which mystery plays were performed in the churches and later, in the thirteenth century, moved out into the streets and public places.

'Father Christmas' had evolved by the reign of Edward III (1327–77) as a character in the play about St George and the Dragon. None of the original text remains but the words have been passed down almost unaltered to the present and the play is still performed at village fetes. 'Father Christmas' is the chorus and 'doubles' as the doctor.

> Here come I, old Father Christmas
> welcome or welcome not
> I hope old Father Christmas
> will never be forgot.

As the play ends he reappears, begging bowl in hand and says:

> Now ladies and gentlemen your sport is just ended,
> So prepare for the box which is highly commended,
> The Box it would speak if it had but a tongue,
> Come throw in your money and think it no wrong.

Throughout Europe in the Middle Ages the most widespread and energetically celebrated event was that of the Feast of Fools, just after Christmas. It was a direct descendant of the Roman

Kalends and was just as depraved, especially in France where the priests and minor clergy who organised it were mostly ill-educated men from peasant stock who had taken with them into the Church many of the rural rituals upon which they had been fed as children.

The Feast of Fools was first described by Johannes Belethus, Rector of Theology in Paris, at the end of the twelfth century, though it was probably celebrated in Constantinople as early as the ninth century.

In 1445 a letter to the Bishops of France from the Paris Faculty of Theology said:

> Priests and clerks may be seen wearing masks and monstrous visages at the hours of office. They dance in choir, dressed as women, pandas or minstrels. They sing wanton songs, they eat black puddings at the horn of the altar while the celebrant is saying Mass. They place dice there. They sense with stinking smoke from the soles of old shoes. They run and leap through the church without a blush at their own shame. Finally they drive about the town and its theatres in shabby carts and rouse the laughter of their fellows and bystanders in infamous performances with indecent gestures and verses scurrilous and unchaste.

The Feast of Fools is a rather shocking reminder that ordinary men need a vehicle for letting down their hair or, as Mr E. Chambers, the Victorian academic, put it rather more eruditely, the feast was 'an ebullition of the lout beneath the cassock'.

An abbot or a bishop was elected to preside over the goings-on. In Scotland, he was called the Abbot of Unreason, like the King of Saturnalia, or the later Lord of Misrule – all in their way a personification of the spirit of the season just like Father Christmas and Santa Claus today.

Children had no part at all in the mediaeval Christmas programme. It was a strictly 'X certificate' affair. The only concession to them at all were the celebrations at Childermas

The Lord of Misrule

or the Feast of the Holy Innocents on 28 December. These were known as the Boy Bishop ceremonies. They were a rather more British, toned-down version of the Feast of Fools and were considerably less bawdy. As long ago as the tenth century a boy was chosen from the cathedral and church choirs to be vested in a cope and mitre and for the short time of his elevation was permitted to give benediction. The 'Bishop' was accompanied by pint-sized archdeacons and canons all dressed for the part and they were entitled to demand supper from their Dean. What a thrill it must have been for the lads whose mediaeval school life was extremely rigorous and for whom holidays were almost unknown.

These ceremonies were so popular that by the late middle ages nearly every parish in the country elected a 'Bishop', until these activities were finally suppressed by Henry VIII in 1541 with the command that 'All such superstitions be lost and clyerly extinguished throughowte.' But tradition dies hard. At the Eton Montem in the 1700s the boys elected a 'priest' to read prayers and another to officiate as a clerk – they were kicked down the hill when it was over! George III loved to attend with the Royal Family and enjoyed it all enormously.

The revelry continued now on its totally secular way and the Lord of Misrule became a familiar figure at Court. Soon every manor house and university appointed its own Lord to oversee the flamboyant events. Very often he was dressed in elaborate and expensive costume. In 1561 in London, Henry Machyn described how ordinary folk watched as the Lord of Misrule rode through London in a 'clear, complete harness, gilt with a hundred great horses and gentlemen riding gorgeously with chains of gold.'

George Ferrers who was a Lord of Misrule for Henry VII ran up a bill of £51 for his outfit.

For Christmas day and that week, the Lord of Misrule himself had a robe of white bawdekyn, containing nine yards at 16s. a yard, garded with a great embroidered gard of cloth of gold, wrought in knots, fourteen yards, at 13s. 4d. a yard, having a fur of red feathers, with a cape of chamblet thrum. A coat of flat silver fine with works, five yards at 50 shillings, with an embroidered gard of leaves of gold and silk coloured, containing fifteen yards at 20 shillings. A cap of maintenance of red feathers and chamblett thrum, very rich, with a plume of feathers. A pair of hosen, the breeches made of a garde of cloth of gold embroidered in paynes, nine yards of gardind at 13s. 4d. lined with silver sarsnet, one ell at 8 shillings. A pair of buskins of white bawdekyn, one yard, at 16 shillings. A pair of pantacles of brydges [Bruges] sattin, 3s. 4d. A girdle of yellow sarsnet, 16d. The cost £51 : 17 : 4.*

Archaeologicia, vol. XVIII.

The post of Lord was often greatly abused – and their powers allowed to run amok. The father of the diarist, Richard Evelyn, defined the duties of his Lord of Misrule at Wotton:

> Imprimis, I give free leave to Owen Flood, my trumpeter, gentleman, to be Lord of Misrule of all good orders during the twelve days. And also, I give free leave to the said Owen Flood to command all and every person or persons whatsoever, as well servants as others, to be at his command whensoever he shall sound his trumpet or music, and to do him good service, as though I were present myself, at their perils . . . I give full power and authority to his lordship to break up all locks, bolts, bars, doors, and latches, and to fling up all doors out of hinges, to come at those who presume to disobey his lordship's commands. God save the King!

During most of this time the Father Christmas figure appears to have lain low. In Scotland after the Reformation, Christmas itself was attacked by the puritanical John Knox and the Nativity ceased to be a major church festival.

But in the rest of the country it was still a time for profligate spending and entertaining, especially amongst the wealthy. The poorer people had to make do with itinerant entertainments, carols and 'gud spice stewe and roste and plum pies for a king' wrote William Warner of the north country during the 1550s.

Present-giving was extremely common and in fact at the beginning of the sixteenth century some people even kept Christmas books to record their gifts! Queen Elizabeth in particular had a liking for personal gifts. Very personal! For in 1579 she was sent a satin night-gown by Sir Francis Walsingham and a green satin petticoat from John Wolley. Tenants gave gifts to landlords; apprentices called on masters for their Christmas 'boxes' which could not be opened without being broken to bits – usually on the day after Christmas. Most of the gift-giving had an ulterior motive and no one bothered much about the children – so Father Christmas was still without work.

The Vindication of
CHRISTMAS,
OR,
His Twelve Yeares Observations upon the

Times, concerning the lamentable Game called Sweep-
stake ; acted by General *Plunder*, and Major General *Tax*;
With his Exhortation to the people ; a description of that
oppressing Ringworm called *Excize* ; and the manner how
our high and mighty Christmas-Ale that formerly would
knock down *Hercules*, & trip up the heels of a Giant, strook
into a deep Consumption with a blow from *Westminster*.

Keep out, you come not here,

O Sir, I bring good cheere.

Old Christmas welcome ; Do not fear.

Imprinted at London for G. Horton, 1653.

He continued to appear in mummers' plays and in 1616 he took the 'lead' in Ben Jonson's play *The Christmas Masque* which is an excellent summary of the Englishman's Christmas in the reign of King James. Mr Gregory Christmas is the father of ten children; Misrule, Minced Pies, Wassail, Carol, etc. There is no Mrs Christmas and he somehow sums up the transition period, from the antics of the Catholic Boy Bishops to the Reformed Church, on the eve of the Puritan revolt: 'I am old Gregory Christmas still, and though I have come out of Pope's head alley, as good a Protestant as any in my Parish.'

In 1632 Willam Prynne complained in his book *Histriomastix*: 'If Turks and Infidels were to behold the Bacchanalian Christmas extravagances, would they not think our Saviour to be a glutton, an epicure, a wine-bibber, a devil, a friend of publicans and sinners?' All such extravagance was finally stopped by Cromwell in 1649. In 1652 it was reported in a broadsheet, *Mercurius Democritus*, that 'Old Christmas is now come to town though few do him regard.' Certainly to all intents and purposes Christmas Day was hardly observed publicly under the Puritans.

The theme in 1652 of the Vindication of Christmas, one of the Thomason Tracts in the British Library, is the rejection of Father Christmas and his failure to find anyone to take him in until eventually he found a remote farmhouse in Devon where the old customs were still observed . . . 'without profaneness or obscenity'. He describes how after dinner they drank lambs-wool (a mixture of ale or cider and puréed apple), chatted, danced, sang or played cards, 'the poor toyling wretches being glad of my company because they had little or no sport at all till I came amongst them. Therefore they skipped and leapt for joy, singing a carol to the tune of Ley – ''Let's dance and sing and make good cheer – For Christmas comes but once a year''.'

When King Charles returned to the throne in 1660 people were once again free to celebrate or worship as they wished, but somehow Christmas did not regain its mediaeval fervour. There was feasting and merrymaking, especially amongst the wealthy but the twenty-fifth was not an excuse for great national merrymaking, and Father Christmas himself seems almost to disappear from the scene.

David Garrick introduced him to an enthusiastic audience in 1774 at Drury Lane, when he staged a musical *A Christmas Tale*, which began with the words 'Behold a personage well known to fame, once loved and honoured – Christmas is my name.'

To a large extent the disappearance of Christmas was accelerated by the growing pains of the Industrial Revolution which began in the mid 1700s – and especially the drastic reduction in the number of annual holidays. By the beginning of the nineteenth century most people were allowed only one day off at Christmas – certainly the days of prolonged merrymaking were over. Moreover, men and women being paid piecework could not afford the time off, since wages were generally very low.

Christmas was in decline; but it was by no means dead. In 1827, just before the great Victorian revival, Charles Lamb wrote: 'Old Christmas is coming. He commeth not with his wonted gait, he is shrunk nine inches in girth but yet he is a lusty fellow.'

THE CHILDREN'S CHRISTMAS

When Queen Victoria came to the throne in 1837 Great Britain and Christmas were ready for a change of heart. In the early years of her reign, the Industrial Revolution began to pay off; the country and the people became gradually more prosperous and there was a resurgence of religious and reforming zeal.

The Queen and her consort, Albert, set a pattern for Christian family life that more people were aware of because more people saw them. Victoria loved the new trains and travelled extensively so the royal progress was reported widely for the first time in the press.

Also, having been ignored, or worse, exploited as fodder for factories, mines or farms, children now became the objects of sympathy and concern. By the late Victorian–Edwardian period, childhood was a near holy state and, though it took time, by the end of the reign Christmas was transformed into the cosy fireside festival we think of nostalgically today as 'how it *ought* to be' – sleigh bells, robins, mistletoe, holly and yule logs, carol singers gathered around their lanterns in the snow, woolly mufflers and Midnight Mass. But, above all, letters to Father Christmas and the excitement of hanging up the stockings on Christmas Eve.

In 1837, in England, Father Christmas was still a little-fêted pagan relic and as the Christmas spirit revived he was increasingly portrayed as a bacchanalian reveller, glass in hand – a jovial yet rather sinister underworld character. Then, as Christianity got the upper hand, he seemed to hover in the shadowy lands between Heaven and Hell – portrayed often as a near-blasphemous representation of Christ Himself, carrying a cross, wearing a thorny crown of holly. No one seemed sure who, or what, he was. He appeared in *The Illustrated London News* as a god-like figure, floating on a cloud, above a host of worshipping pilgrims and animals. He appeared in *Punch* with a bunch of nude lovelies on the beach. A figurehead was obviously needed to represent the spirit of Christmas but should he belong to the Christian revival or to the increasingly prosperous capitalist world? It took the Americans to make the decision.

When America was first colonised in the sixteenth and seventeenth centuries European settlers took with them many of

A pre-Nast version of St Nicholas

their national Christmas personalities and traditions. As in Europe, these thrived on a regional basis. Befana from Italy, the Christkindl from Germany, the Three Wise Men from Spain – all were known as gift-bearers. Father Christmas was there too, from Britain – but was a very minor figure. In New Amsterdam the Dutch celebrated the festival of Sinterklaas, their beloved patron.

No one knows how, or why, the transformation happened. A complex change of social and economic circumstances made it possible, but why 'Santa Claus' suddenly emerged as a Christmas 'star' – who can say?

The very first known written description of the character we know today appeared in Washington Irving's *Knickerbocker's History of New York* in 1809 – not, as is usually claimed, in 1823 when Clement C. Moore's poem 'The Visit of St Nicholas' was published.

The good St Nicholas would often make his appearance in his beloved city of a holiday afternoon, riding jollily above the tree tops or over the roofs of the houses, now and then drawing forth magnificent presents from his breeches pockets and dropping them down the chimneys of his favourites. Whereas in these degenerate days of iron and brass he never visits us save one night in the year when he rattles down the chimneys of the descendants of patriarchs, confining his presents merely to the children in token of the degeneracy of the parents.

This description of St Nicholas had clearly made an impression on Mr Irving – but who told it to him? All we can deduce is that St Nicholas lost his cope and mitre in some places and crossed the boundaries of folklore well before 1809. The symbolism of the shaman, of Saturn and Odin and Sinterklaas were coming together.

Irving's book appeared fourteen years, then, before the publication of Clement C. Moore's famous poem.

T'was the night before Christmas, when all through the house
Not a creature was stirring, not even a mouse;
The stockings were hung by the chimney with care,
In hopes that St Nicholas soon would be there;
The children were nestled all snug in their beds,
While visions of sugar-plums danced in their heads;
And Mamma in her kerchief, and I in my cap,
Had just settled our brains for a long winter's nap,
When out on the lawn there arose such a clatter,
I sprang from the bed to see what was the matter,
Away to the window I flew like a flash,
Tore open the shutters and threw up the sash.
The moon on the breast of the new-fallen snow
Gave the lustre of midday to objects below,
When, what to my wondering eyes should appear,
But a miniature sleigh, and eight tiny reindeer,
With a little old driver, so lively and quick,
I knew in a moment it must be St Nick.
More rapid than eagles his coursers they came,
And he whistled, and shouted, and called them by name:
Now, Dasher! now Dancer! now Prancer and Vixen!
On, Comet! on, Cupid! on, Donner and Blitzen!
To the top of the porch! to the top of the wall!
Now dash away! dash away! dash away all!
As dry leaves that before the wild hurricane fly,
When they meet with an obstacle, mount to the sky,
So up to the house-top the coursers they flew,
With the sleigh full of toys, and St Nicholas too.
And then, in a twinkling, I heard on the roof
The prancing and pawing of each little hoof,
As I drew in my head, and was turning around,
Down the chimney St Nicholas came with a bound.
He was dressed all in fur, from his head to his foot,
And his clothes were all tarnished with ashes and soot;
A bundle of toys he had flung on his back,

And he looked like a pedlar just opening his pack.
His eyes – how they twinkled! his dimples how merry!
His cheeks were like roses, his nose like a cherry!
His droll little mouth was drawn up like a bow,
And the beard of his chin was as white as the snow;
The stump of a pipe he held tight in his teeth,
And the smoke it encircled his head like a wreath;
He had a broad face and a little round belly,
That shook when he laughed, like a bowlful of jelly.
He was chubby and plump, a right jolly old elf,
And I laughed when I saw him, in spite of myself;
A wink of his eye and a twist of his head
Soon gave me to know I had nothing to dread.
He spoke not a word, but went straight to his work,
And filled all the stockings; then turned with a jerk,
And laying his finger aside of his nose,
And giving a nod, up the chimney he rose;
He sprang to his sleigh, to his team gave a whistle,
And away they all flew like the down of a thistle.
But I heard him exclaim, ere he drove out of sight,
'Happy Christmas to all and to all a good night.'

Clement C. Moore was a professor of Hebrew and Greek at
the Episcopalian Theological College, New York. He wrote the
poem on the evening of 3 December 1822 for the amusement
of his own children and it is the only work by which he is
remembered. Yet he was so ashamed of it that when a lady
friend sent it to the *Troy Sentinel* for publication the following
year, he refused to acknowledge authorship. In fact, not until
1838, by which time the poem was a national favourite, did he
admit that it was his work.

He was right. It is *not* a great poem, but it did fix firmly in the
American mind the new image of a tiny, jovial figure in a tunic
of fur, riding through the night not on a white horse but, for the
first time, on a reindeer-driven sleigh. All that remained for

most people of the venerable St Nicholas of Myra was the American version of his name – 'Santa Claus'. It was rather like a local lad being discovered and groomed out of recognition as a pop star by his PR so that he becomes hardly recognisable to the folks back home – and the Dutch didn't like him.

Quite a bit later, in the 1860s, the well-known artist Thomas Nast produced a series of drawings for the *Harpers Illustrated Weekly* which finally brought Moore's poem to life. The Dutch continued to celebrate St Nicholas Day with the saint, in a red tunic, on horseback. But it was Nast's secular, entirely benevolent Santa Claus which caught the imagination of the nation and was very soon to be shipped back across the ocean to Europe.

Meanwhile in Britain (though not in puritanical Scotland or in Ireland) the Victorian Christmas was gathering momentum. In 1837 Dickens published *Pickwick Papers* with its Christmas at Dingley Dell, followed in 1843 by *A Christmas Carol* in which the Spirit of Christmas Present is illustrated by a bare-chested 'Bacchus'. This is not Father Christmas – but in Dickens's mind he clearly belongs to the same family:

> It was clothed in one simple green robe or mantle, bordered with white fur. This garment hung so loosely on the figure that its capacious breast was bare, as if disdaining to be warded or concealed by any artifice. Its feet, observable beneath the ample folds of the garment were also bare, and on its head it wore no other covering than a holly wreath, set here and there with shining icicles. Its dark brown curls were long and free; free as its genial face, its sparkling eye, its cheery voice, its open hand, its unconstrained demeanour and its joyful air. Girded round its middle was an antique scabbard; but no sword was in it and the ancient sheath was eaten up with rust.

A Christmas Carol stressed the new idea of an obligation to see that children had a good and happy time and Prince Albert himself set the example by popularising in 1843 the Christmas

A Victorian greetings card showing the blurred boundaries between the pagan and Christian celebration of Christmas. *Mary Evans Picture Library*

tree around which the huge royal family gathered on Christmas morning.

Dickens was a zealous self-publicist and he set about promoting *A Christmas Carol* with almost evangelical fervour – with such success that by 1844 over 15,000 copies had been sold, at a time when most people did not buy many books or have access to libraries.

The new breed of industrialist saw enormous money-making potential in the ideas propagated by Dickens. Both in the Christmas festival and in children themselves they recognised opportunities for big business. Many people were better off; it should not be too difficult to persuade them to lavish a little of their new affluence on the festive season, especially to please the little ones.

Present-giving was still confined largely to the wealthy – Prince Albert thought it was a 'pretty custom', and most gifts were given – as they were in Europe – on New Year's Day.

There was a certain amount of individual present-giving

between members of families but it was on a very limited scale and the commercial steamrollering of the public into near compulsory and profligate generosity was still 150 years away.

The seeds were being sown by the 1850s and descriptions in *The Illustrated London News* vividly record Christmas preparations in the London stores. There is talk of butchers, poulterers, fruiterers, grocers but as yet no mention of toy shops, or manufactured decorations.

Christmas preparations certainly did not begin until Christmas week itself and in 1856 Nathaniel Hawthorne, the American writer, commented that on 20 December shops in London were beginning to 'show some tokens of approaching Christmas'. When presents were purchased they were given personally and not by Father Christmas – he had not yet appeared in Britain with his bottomless sack of surprises.

In 1883 Max O'Rell described the English Christmas to the French – and he certainly talks of Father Christmas 'avec sa longue barbe couverte de frumas, descend par la cheminée pour remplir de bonbons et de joux les bas que les enfants ont suspendu au pied du lit'. He obviously thought the custom widespread, which is strange because only a few years before, in 1879, there was a puzzled letter in the journal *Notes and Queries* from a member of the Folklore Society:

I have not seen the following observance recorded anywhere' and having been only lately told of it by a country person cognizant of its observance both in Herefordshire and Worcestershire from personal knowledge reaching up to last year perhaps in addition to other folk lore it may be worth a place in *Notes and Queries*.

On Christmas Eve, when the inmates of the house in the country retire to bed, all those desirous of a present place a stocking outside the door of their bedroom, with the expectation that some mythical being called Santiclaus will fill the stocking or place something within it before the morning. This is of course well known and the master of the house does in reality place a Christmas gift secretly in each stocking; but the giggling girls in the morning, when bringing down their presents, affect to say that Santiclaus visited and filled the stockings in the night. From what region of the earth or air this benevolent Santiclaus takes flight I have not been able to ascertain but probably he may be heard of in other countries than those I have mentioned. An Exeter resident tells me this custom prevails also in Devonshire.

We know – even if the writer of the letter, the sceptical Mr Lees, did not – that the benevolent visitor had arrived from America. The confusion of the two characters had begun.

The British Father Christmas still existed in his own right – but gradually his personality was changing, as his role of a gift-bringer began. W. Webb wrote *Jack and the Beanstalk*, the toy theatre play based on a pantomime at Drury Lane in which the old Father Christmas had a role. In the early 1860s Pollocks' Toy Theatre Company designed one of their famous sets based on this pantomime. The Pollocks' Father Christmas is a gentler, toned-down character, designed to appeal to children. He now wears a red, fur-trimmed gown and a wreath of holly and sits beaming kindly over a Christmas table on which stands the inevitable wassail bowl.

Later, in 1913, the March issue of a magazine called *The Mask* published an article on 'The Webb Juvenile Drama' by D. R. Francis Eagle, which states:

A masterpiece of the juvenile theatre, Webb's pantomime Jack and the Beanstalk or The Pranks of the Good Little Fairies in 27 delightful plates of characters and scenery. The scenes picture the twelve months of the year, six scenes allowing for the development of the story and the remainder give a rollicking . . . harlequinade concluding with the scene of The Hall of Happy Old Christmas; needless to say the fairies are in full force in this scene and our old friends, clown, Pantaloon, Harlequin and Columbine well to the front.

Father Christmas and friends by Thomas Nast. *Mary Evans Picture Library*

Stores in America and Canada had introduced Santa Claus as early as the 1860s and in Britain, too, Christmas grottoes were created to house him.

B. Hyam, a national hatter, tailor, outfitter, clothier and hosier, most unusually took a whole column in the *Manchester Guardian* in verse:

First of all throughout the globe
Does Hyam take his stand
To welcome Christmas with Eclat
And take him by the hand.
And 61 now finds him right
And ready for the mass
With wondrous dress in great excess
To suit each varied class.

In 1886 a magazine called simply *Illustrated Bits* acclaimed:

Look. Look. Look. Grand monster Santa Claus surprise
parcels. Each parcel contains: 12 very handsome and choice
Christmas and New Year Cards of new and original designs;
4 beautiful coloured Christmas mottos suitable for decorations; 1 fine silver-plated thimble, enamelled inside; 1 fine
steel pocket knife with bone handle; 1 leatherette writing
case and companion (everybody needs this); 1 bijou draught
board and set of draughts; 1 24-note celestial tone harmonica;
1 book of Language of the Flowers Precious Stones; 1 gold-
plated representation Spade Guinea suitable for watch charm
or pendant; 1 gold or silver-plated stem winding toy watch
charm or chain – the child's delight; 1 magic frog or spider;
1 universal patent mechanograph; pictures; designs; maps;
plans; 1 child's nursery tale book . . . Just think . . . we will
send the entire parcel post paid to any address in the UK for
2s 9d, two parcels for 5s 3d or three parcels for 7s 6d.

So, as advertisements urged people to spend and, most
practically important, the post office offered an improved
parcel post, there inevitably followed a need for someone
special to deliver the goods. Who better than the genial child
lover, the American Santa Claus? Around 1890 old Father
Christmas was finally stripped of his holly crown and flask of
wine and became the clean-living, almost saintly benefactor we
love today.

SUPER-SANTA

Like the mortals to whom he comes, the twentieth-century Father Christmas is a much-travelled character. Victorian explorers had opened up the world, missionaries and settlers migrated to faraway places, aeroplanes took off and soon the whole world was on the move. Advertising and the television caught up with the energetic red-coated figure on the sleigh and before long he was familiar to Red Indians, Aborigines, Maoris and Africans, not as a saint but as a provider of goodies. His origins were completely forgotten. In the minds of most people in Europe and the United States Father Christmas and Santa Claus became one and the same. He was often called Santa Claus but he was *really* Father Christmas.

At the turn of the century Santa turned up wearing Father Christmas clothes in a Montreal store exhibition, where he was shown talking to a kangaroo in Australia, shipwrecked in Patagonia, meeting Kitchener in South Africa, chatting to Teddy Roosevelt and finally riding whaleback up the St Lawrence to Montreal.

This new mixed-up 'Santa Christmas' or 'Father Claus' was seen arriving on snow shoes, by water skis, even by camel. He appeared on early Christmas cards and was posted to friends abroad. He was on the cover of the famous *Pears Soap Annual* in 1893 long before 'Bubbles' made her debut.

In Canada he stayed young by drinking Bovril. In Britain it was chocolate. In America he was put on trial in the famous case of Santa Claus (inc.) Oshkosh *v* Santa Claus (inc.) Omaha, when rival companies disputed the trade use of his name.

He entertained the troops in the trenches during the First World War and visited Princess Elizabeth and Princess

Margaret Rose during the thirties when, as all Royal children still do, they hung up their stockings.

In 1939 'Rudolph', the red-nosed reindeer, joined the team.

Throughout most of this time Father Christmas was closer to his young admirers than he had ever been. He was *real* – he rode through the skies in his reindeer-drawn sleigh, toy sack bulging – just like Mummy and Daddy said. And deep down inside, Mummy and Daddy shared the fantasies. The big bad world of business did not yet greatly intrude on the nursery.

Not till after the Second World War did the commercial bandwagon really start rolling, and Father Christmas became a tool of trade. He was well and truly groomed for the Mickey Mouse merchandising treatment. He became a super salesman – and the spotlight of so much international attention, sadly, banished some of the mystery but not quite all. In a society that relies on synthetics he is now inevitably a mass-produced, often synthetic character. Like most figureheads he is a mirror of his times. His role may have changed today but he clearly still has a part to play. Grown-ups just can't do without him, and children are happy to accept him as he is. So what is he up to?

The season in London starts around February when Bermans, the theatrical costumiers – founded in 1900 as a military tailors – begin to hire their 200 Santa Claus and Father Christmas costumes to photographic studios for the November–December advertising campaigns. For £20 a week plus VAT they offer 'Father Christmas' outfits (recommended for slimfits) – a slipover red, fur-trimmed 'dressing gown' with an attached pointed hood, or 'Santa Claus' gear (for portly gentlemen) – a baggy, loose jacket with a black belt, pantaloons and a nightcap with a pom-pom.

Business is brisk all year but the hangers are cleared again nearer to Christmas with the advent of charity bazaars and fetes where Father Christmas is a big money-raiser.

But, of course, most of the Berman business since the firm's

41

The sleigh-drawn Santa

foundation has been concerned with the Fairy Grotto sections of departmental stores. This is changing in Britain for fewer and fewer departmental stores can afford the space that a Grotto occupies – and many of those who do are sadly forced to charge an admission fee.

Not so Harrods, where they do things in style. One of a team of *three* Father Christmasses – chosen for their similar height – sits on a golden chair to receive visitors, for free. Mind you, they don't get a present either.

'We have to have a rota system because they got so tired shaking all those hands and chatting to all the Mums – the children don't notice,' a spokesman from Harrods says.

Selfridges don't suffer from this problem. Their Father Christmas, they say, is 'the real one – tireless'. A special contract was drawn up with him just before the last war and he has been stopping off in Oxford Street ever since. Just imagine – 16,000 hands to shake each Saturday and about 10,000 each weekday from November to December. That's a total of about three quarters of a million. In addition to all that he has a fan mail of 3,400 letters to deal with. Super-Santa indeed.

All these goings-on have thoroughly upset the American-born naturalised Englishman who calls himself the Super-Santa – founder of the Father Xmas Union (The Brotherhood of Father Christmas and Santa Claus).

Mr Ed Berman, whose other activities range from creating City Farms to staging Tom Stoppard's plays in London's West End, and whose entry in *Who's Who* occupies a whole page, is a fervent defender of childhood. He is very upset by the sight of boys and girls conveyor-belted through papier-mâché fairylands. This is why he founded the Union in 1969 as a ginger group whose aim is 'to protect the fantasies of children from exploitation of a commercial, political and religious nature'. (How about the fantasies of grown-ups too?) His avowed intent is to picket the big stores and to banish grotto Santas for ever. 'The FXU is a Mafia for Good,' he claims darkly. 'We have members,

43

worldwide, infiltrating stores, organisations and even Parliaments, all determined to bring back a little joy. Why should this most wonderful of all myths be reduced to tat and doddering old fools.'

Mind you, Mr Berman, 'twas ever thus! In 1897 George Bernard Shaw wrote 'Christmas is forced on a reluctant and disgusted nation by shopkeepers and the press.'

And as late as 1957 in France a group of churchmen weren't at all happy with Father Christmas in any form. The newspaper *France Soir* reported:

Father Christmas was hanged yesterday from the railings of Dijon Cathedral and burned publicly in the precinct. This spectacular execution took place in the presence of several hundred children from the Sunday Schools. It was decided with the agreement of the clergy who had condemned Father Christmas as a usurper and a heretic. He was accused of paganising the festival of Christmas and installing himself like a cuckoo, taking up more and more room. Above all he was accused of infiltrating State schools from which the crib has been banished.

In a way, Mr Berman is himself rather like a kindly Roman king of Saturnalia harking back to a mythical Golden Age – only with any luck he won't have to die for his cause!

Besides, a child's imagination is tougher than you'd think. They mostly understand that the jolly old chap with sweaty hands in the chain store, who charges 50p for a peep at his tatty cottonwool beard, is not the *real* Father Christmas. Although they are tele-bred and worldly wise they still cling to their belief in the night-flying philanthropist and probably always will.

THE GRAND TOUR

In many regions the gentle St Nicholas and the traditional spirits of the night – Befana the witch, Knecht Ruprecht – have retreated into the shadows from which they came. The impact of the all-American energetic stereotype has been enormous. He has even turned up on mainland China with the name of Lang Khoong (nice old father) or Dunche Lao (Christmas old man). But the takeover is not total. Sometimes they live happily side by side. But whoever children – and grown-up children – believe will visit them during the night of 24/25 December, or at New Year or on 6 December, people everywhere look forward to those magical days of midwinter when they can all share the 'willing suspension of disbelief'.

The American Christmas is as expansive and varied as the country itself. The country which created Santa Christmas has gone characteristically overboard with its exaggerated portrayal of his personality. In America he is brasher, brighter, more versatile, more sentimenal and perhaps less believable than anywhere else. However, there are still pockets of the country where the old European rituals are clung to, and during December the celestial traffic lanes are busy with nightriders in the sky – Sinterklaas, Ru Nikolas (the American form of Knecht Ruprecht), Befana, the Three Wise Men all passing by.

Needless to say, grown-up Americans freely acknowledge their love of childish things – they revel in simple fun and games. It is therefore not surprising to find that there is a place called Santa Claus and a village named North Pole. Santa Claus is a small town in Indiana which handles 3,000,000 letters each

Variations on the theme

Christmas. It is said that in 1882 the residents of the new, un-named community were gathered in the Post Office on Christmas Eve when Santa Claus walked in, and they agreed to name their settlement after him. Now the Post Office is a museum and on Kriss Kringle Street there is a 23 inch coloured statue of Santa Claus. The college offers students a BSC – Bachelor in Santa Clausery – and the Chamber of Commerce in Santa Claus issues a guide for anyone intending to play the role at Christmas. There is a chapter on 'Talking with Children' which wisely warns 'Under no circumstances talk to a child with alcohol on your breath for this damages the character of Santa Claus the world over.' There is information on how to make a beard from yak hair and thin Santas are advised 'do not use a pillow stuffing . . . but a more systematic method of placing . . . a one or two inch foam rubber layer up underneath the arms and down to the waist'. The pamphlet concludes with a useful list of do's and don't's:

Do : Be jolly, Be friendly, Be firm, Be alert

Don't : Be gruff, Fall asleep while on the job, Drink, smoke or chew on the job, Threaten children to be good, Accept money from a parent in front of the child.

On route 431 in New York State 13 miles from Lake Placid and high in the Whiteface Mountain is the village of North Pole (zip code 12946). There, on the site of the 1980 Winter Olympics, is Santa's Workshop – a winter Disneyland, described in the brochure as a 'family oriented resort'. Here, in 1946, Art Monaco – late of the Walt Disney organisation – designed a log cabin village containing a post office, blacksmith's forge, chapel, and toy workshops. It is now, like all things American, a high-powered efficiently run holiday centre . . . and it has a press office to put you in the picture, and operates package tours.

Santa's house is the centre of the village. There he sits in his rocking chair beside a boxful of lollipops opposite a grandfather clock, which is a camera in disguise taking happy family snapshots of young visitors chatting happily. There is a Reindeer Barn – and rides in a sleigh, of course; magic shows; a ride up and down a giant Christmas tree; and craft shops galore where artists blow glass, make candies, carve wood.

In the middle of all this jollity is a Nativity Pageant performed on a flower-covered hillside. For, of course, to make it pay Santa's Workshop is open to tourists from May to October after which Santa sets out on his travels . . . to return just in time for a special Christmas Preview weekend when families may stay as Santa's guests (paying) for four days' action-packed Christmas activity.

Being Father Christmas in Australia is a hot and sweaty business – for 25 December falls in midsummer, yet every department store has its fairy grotto. Keeping Christmas alive down under has meant a really nostalgic determination, for the fundamental purpose of the original midwinter festival seems a little remote in a country where the December sun shines for weeks on end and temperatures soar to 100°F in the shade. Nevertheless Australians celebrate the holiday today with the Dickensian enthusiasm of the Victorians in the old country . . . with turkey, plum pudding and crackers. True, there is a move these days to pack up a picnic and migrate for the day to the beach, but it is no ordinary picnic. Cold turkey, steaks, salads, exotic fruits together with plenty of chilled wines and beers abound.

Tradition dies hard and wherever there are children in Australia, Father Christmas will find them. He has arrived on Bondai beach by boat; he has skied down the Nerang river wearing only a white beard and bright red trunks; he has landed by plane in the outback where there are more shepherds watching their flocks than anywhere in the Holy Land.

The Austrian postal service sets up a special office in the village of Christkindl to answer children's letters addressed, not to Santa Claus, but to the Lord Jesus (provided they enclose a s.a.e.).

Of all the places that Father Christmas probably does *not* visit, the oddest must be Australia's Christmas Island, in the Indian Ocean . . . whose only claim to fame is the quality of its bird droppings! Scientifically known as guano, they yield important phosphates which are extracted by the tiny multi-race community. On 25 December 1777 Captain Cook discovered an uninhabited island, called it 'Christmas Island', and said that it had 'one of the most inhospitable climates in the world'.

The Finnish Father Christmas lives in Lapland. His home is atop Korvantunturi, a 483-metre hill at Savukoski on the eastern border with the Arctic Circle. His name – Joulupukki – means, literally, the Christmas Goat, for the goat was a sacrificial animal in pagan times, and has always had mystical importance in many lands. At one time gifts were always given anonymously and thrown through the window – later they were labelled with the recipients' names and a horned figure, similar to the masked dancers of Kalends, acted as 'Father Christmas'. Later still, that rather grotesque gift-bringer turned human and became St Nicholas, though he was still called Joulupukki and arrives not on St Nicholas Eve but on 24 December.

Each year the Finnish Joulupukki receives letters from children all over the world. These days he has to call on the services of a team of government-paid translating 'elves' who reply in English, German, French, Dutch, Japanese, Spanish and Italian.

In 1979 there were over 40,000 such communications. Each child was sent a cheerful airmail letter accompanied by a coloured photograph of Joulupukki with his reindeer, and containing a simple puzzle.

The North Pole Village

Through the kindness of the Post Office, Finnish children may even telephone to Savukoski to place their Christmas present orders!

In Germany there are many variations on the gift-bringer theme, most of them ancient, and as sinister as the pinewoods of the Black Forest. Nowhere has Christianity been more confused with the forces of darkness. Probably the two best-known figures are the Christkindl and the terrible Knecht Ruprecht.

The Christkindl is not so old and was developed in the early seventeenth century as an attempt by the Protestant church to substitute Christ for the allegedly popish St Nicholas. It seems that parents had, even then, been telling their children that St Nicholas would bring them gifts. Once again the original concept was worked on by time and overactive imaginations, and so a Christ-child figure was evolved to replace him. The Christkindl went to America in the eighteenth century with German settlers and became Kriss Kringle – a kind of mythical angel messenger riding a donkey and bringing presents. Inevitably he became confused with Santa Claus. In Germany today's Christkindl bears little resemblence to his holy inspiration, and often the part is played by a girl (yet another legacy from Kalends), wearing a white gown with a veil and a star on her head, who leaves presents on Christmas Eve. In Nuremberg a Christkindl is elected every Christmas.

On the other hand the Knecht Ruprecht is a sinister throwback to the nightmarish world of the bogyman. Knecht Ruprecht, looking a little like Odin, in an outfit of fur or straw and with a long, red tongue and wild eyes was a frightful partner for St Nicholas on his travels. The Knecht Ruprecht belonged to the mountainside and dark nights and carried a stick to beat naughty children who did not know their prayers.

Today that stick often has a present attached to its end and parents no longer frighten their children with horror stories.

But Knecht Ruprecht is still there at the side of the Weihnachts-mann – the Christmas Man. In German towns, the Weihnachts-mann wears the trappings of Santa Claus and looks much the same as Santa anywhere – but in the rural areas, St Nicholas in his mitre is hanging on and has not yet been deposed.

Neither Santa Claus nor Father Christmas are known in Greece outside Athens for although St Nicholas is the Greek patron saint he has never become a cult figure. Instead the Greeks – grown-ups and children alike – are far more aware and fearful of the terrible Kallikantzaroi who emerge from the bowels of the earth around Christmas time. All year round these hideous creatures are striving to cut away the tree which supports the earth – then just as they have nearly succeeded Christ is born and they leap to the surface in rage. The furious hunt that follows is very like that of the Herlathing hunt which terrorised Norse and Teutonic Europe and quite likely a nightmarish interpretation of what really happened when masked revellers ran amok during the midwinter festivals.

Children born on 25 December are feared to be in danger of becoming one of the Kallikantzaroi and must be bound in straw or garlic tresses.

The usual way of frightening the spirits is with fire, and a special log, hewn from a thorny tree, is brought in (like the 'Yule' log) to burn for the twelve days of Christmas.

Holland is still the stronghold of the real Santa Claus, the direct descendant of St Nicholas of Myra. Father Christmas hardly dares set foot here.

All Dutch children know that Santa Claus lives in Spain where Piet, his little Moorish helper, stocks up on Christmas presents and Santa spends the year recording their behaviour, good and bad, in a little red book. This idea must have arisen from the Spanish occupation of the Netherlands.

On 6 December – St Nicholas Eve – Piet and the saint arrive by boat through the chilly mists of Amsterdam harbour to be greeted by the mayor and most of the townsfolk. It is a magic moment – sheer pageantry free from commercial or, it must be admitted, religious undertones. Sinterklaas rides ashore on his white horse (remember Odin's Sleipir?). He wears a mitre and the resplendent red robes of a bishop and carries a crozier. But his saintly status has long been forgotten and his arrival is celebrated equally in Holland by Jew and Christian alike.

Together Piet and Sinterklaas lead a splendid procession along the old canals of Amsterdam, with children cheering and waving all the way. For them this is just the beginning of the Sinterklaas season.

At home that evening they will feast with their families and exchange gifts. Present-giving in Holland is very different from that in Britain and America. All packets are traditionally camouflaged so that it is impossible to detect the contents. They must then be hidden around the house so that everyone works for their reward by following a treasure trail. Each present is also accompanied by a poem – signed 'Sinterklaas' – which may be long or short but must pick up some harmless gossip or make friendly fun of the recipient. It is all very good humoured since each person must read aloud whatever has been said of him by Sinterklaas. It is an occasion for great family hilarity – a chance, just once a year, to bring blushes to the cheeks of the nearest and dearest.

After the gifts comes the food, and a table on Sinterklaas Eve looks much the same as it did in the seventeenth century when some of the Dutch Old Masters painted the ceremonies. There are still large chocolate initials to mark each place and men and women made of dark brown pastry like gingerbread and called 'speculaas' – 'lovers'.

As the evening comes to an end around midnight and the children are sent up to bed, they put a slipper by the fire filled with hay or a carrot for the horse in the hopes that, if they have been good, Sinterklaas will remember them and leave a gift.

In Iceland it is the goblins Jola Sveinar who take the place of Father Christmas. They have cheerful names like Bowl Licker, Door Smeller and Window Peeper, and they arrive one a day during the week before Christmas, each bringing a gift.

The Feast of St Nicholas is still observed in faithful Italy as a religious rite – there are no graven images in red coats . . . though that is not to say that the whiz kids of commerce don't cash in on Christianity itself!

Strangely, the children of Italy still believe that the good witch, Befana (her name is a corruption of Epiphany), will bring their presents on the eve of 6 January.

The origins of Befana are obscure and may well be pagan, but Italians like to think she was the old lady who directed the Three Wise Men on their way to Bethlehem. Because she was delayed from following them she never managed to find the Christ Child herself and has been searching ever since, delivering gifts as she goes.

To little Russians, their Father Christmas is known as Grandfather Frost and he lives in the little Norwegian town of Budo, though the people of Budo are quite unaware of this. Grandfather Frost arrives in Russia on New Year's Day which has been a major festival since Peter the Great decreed in 1699 that special celebrations should take place at that time.

Grandfather Frost has masses of white hair and a bushy beard just like Father Christmas, but his hat is cossack style and his coat often made entirely of warm fur, too. On his journey from the far north, Grandfather Frost is usually accompanied by the Snow Maiden, daughter of Father Frost and Fairy Spring. Legend says that her cold heart deprived her of human happiness until she learned the meaning of love.

The Snow Maiden, dressed all in white and carrying a glistening wand, speeds through the countryside with him on New Year's Eve placing presents under the freshly cut fir trees which are taken into every home for the festival.

Christmas in Oslo may look much the same as Christmas in London but in the Norwegian countryside people are very jealous of their national folklore.

Today's Julenisse – or Christmas gnome – was once known as the 'haugkallen', a tiny red-capped creature who lived in the barn and protected the farm only so long as he was well looked after. This is why, even today, Norwegian children put out a plate of porridge to prevent him wrecking the homestead.

But as in other parts of Europe the little Norwegian hobgoblin became confused with the figure of St Nicholas. The haugkallen became Jul Nisse (the name Nisse is the old form of Nils or Nicholas) and bore a striking resemblance to the St Nicholas of Clement C. Moore's poem.

In Sweden a similar but kindly gnome is known as the Jultomten. He, too, likes porridge. More recently Father Christmas has taken his place and knocks on the door on Christmas Eve asking 'Are there any kind children here?' But in Denmark the 'Christmas Man' is the only one who is a *real* father. He turns up on Christmas Eve for a dish of rice pudding with all his elf-like offspring.

In Catholic Spain and in the Spanish-speaking countries of South America, Christmas itself is a deeply religious time. Spanish children must wait until the eve of Epiphany – 6 January – for their gifts. That night, they believe, the Three

Wise Men will cross their country bearing gifts, not only for the infant Jesus but for all good children. So they leave out barley and water to feed the camels on their way.

Among the stops made at New Year by Grandfather Frost is Norilsk, on the Taimyr Peninsula. At 68.5°N, Norilsk is one of the most northerly towns in the world. Despite the terrible weather there in the depth of winter, he turns up on his sledge with the Snow Maiden, who accompanies him wherever he goes throughout the New Year festivities. The sun does not rise for the occasion, for here in the Arctic Circle there are six months of daylight and six months of night.

Founded in the mid-thirties as an ore-mining centre, Norilsk is built on piles driven deep into the ground – otherwise the warmth of the buildings might thaw the layer of eternally frozen ground, with dire consequences!

In winter there may be blizzards lasting for two weeks at a stretch, so Grandfather Frost moves for a great deal of the time through covered walkways between the nurseries, schools, children's clubs and the town's Palace of Culture, where he and the Snow Maiden attend a big children's party.

There are other more northerly points which Grandfather Frost visits, because he goes wherever there are children. These include settlements along the Arctic coast, traditionally inhabited by itinerant national minorities such as Eskimos, Nenets and Chukchi. Like Norilsk, they are set among Arctic tundra, in seasonal-looking landscapes, and reindeers are plentifully available to pull Grandfather Frost's sledge.

Midwinter is 23 June in the Antarctic and workers for the British Antarctic Survey celebrate Christmas then in a 24-hour night. Sadly, Father Christmas does not seem to have travelled so far south – though he would be welcome, say the stalwarts at Scott Base.

'DEAR FATHER CHRISTMAS . . .'

Every year millions of little – and not so little – children write to Father Christmas to let him know what they would like best in their stockings on Christmas morning. In some places these letters are 'posted' up the chimney – but mostly they are popped by parents into the letter box on the corner with an astonishing degree of faith, for the imaginary addresses are a supreme test of Post Office ingenuity.

The British Post Office, which has a heart of gold, channels every letter to Father Christmas or Santa Claus in the right direction. There are 250,000 of them each year, heading for – 'North Poal, the Wurld', 'Toyland, Greenland', 'North Pole Alaska', 'The Top of the World', 'Lapland, Finland', 'Reindeer Land', 'Up in the Sky', 'Igloo Number One, Reykjavik Iceland', 'The Toy Shop, Christmas Land', 'Snowland, North Pole'.

In deference to the amount of business he brings them the Post Office have selected a Father Christmas design by five-year-old Samantha Brown from Wales as the 1981 $11\frac{1}{2}$p stamp.

Not surprisingly chain stores too receive sackfuls of Father Christmas mail each year. Harrods' young customers, as might be expected, seem to anticipate a gilt-edged service – one little girl last year asked 'Dear Santa Claus, we are going away for Christmas this year so please could you call and keep my ponies company?'

Both Harrods and Father Christmas should be proud of their international reputation for amongst the requests that arrived last year was a letter from a little boy in Tibet! It was written in wobbly English on thick wallpaper. 'Dear Father Christmas please don't forget me because I live so far away,' it pleaded.

Of course, it is not only children who write to Father Christmas.

Remember Laurent de Brunhoff's Babar the Elephant who told his children how in the human world on Christmas Eve a kind old man with a long, white beard, in a red coat and a pointed cap, travels through the air carrying toys to give to little children, though he is difficult to see for he comes down the chimney while the children are asleep. So Babar encouraged Pom, Flora, Arthur and Alexander to write and ask Father Christmas to come to the land of the elephants too.

But it wasn't as easy as that for the children weren't sure any more than human boys and girls *where* Father Christmas lived. So Babar went off to find him for them.

Eventually he tracked down an old book written in Gothic letters which states that Father Christmas lives in Bohemia in the little town of Prjmnestwe – and that was where Babar eventually found him, living shaman-style in an underground cave.

There was also the tale of King John, as told by A. A. Milne, with decorations by E. H. Shepard.

> King John was not a good man
> And no good friends had he.
> He stayed in every afternoon
> But no one came to tea
> And round about December
> The cards upon his shelf,
> Which wished him lots of Christmas cheer
> And fortune in the coming year
> Were never from his near and dear
> But only from himself.
>
> King John was not a good man
> Yet had his hopes and fears.
> They'd given him no present now
> For years and years and years,

But every year at Christmas
While minstrels stood about
Collecting tribute from the young
For all the songs they might have sung
He stole away upstairs and hung
A hopeful stocking out.

King John was not a good man
He lived his life aloof.
Alone he thought a message out
While climbing on the roof.
He wrote it down and propped it
Against the chimney stack.
'TO ALL AND SUNDRY – NEAR AND FAR –
FATHER CHRISTMAS IN PARTICULAR'
And signed it, not 'Johannes R'
But very humbly 'Jack'.

'We want some crackers
And I want some candy
I think a box of chocolates
Would come in handy,
I don't mind oranges,
I do like nuts
And I SHOULD like a pocket knife
That really cuts.
And Oh! Father Christmas, if you love me at all,
Bring me a big red india rubber ball!'

King John was not a good man.
He wrote this message out
And got him to his room again
Descending by the spout.
And all that night he lay there
A prey to hopes and fears.
I think that's him a-coming now,
(Anxiety bedewed his brow.)
He'll bring one present, anyhow,
The first I've had for years.

'Forget about the crackers
And forget about the candy;
I'm sure a box of chocolates
Would never come in handy;
I don't like oranges,
I don't want nuts,
And I HAVE got a pocket knife
That almost cuts.
But, oh! Father Christmas, if you love me at all,
Bring me a big, red, india-rubber ball!'

King John was not a good man –
Next morning when the sun
Rose up to tell the waiting world
That Christmas had begun
And people seized their stockings
And opened them with glee
And crackers, games and toys appeared
And lips with sticky sweets were smeared,
King John said grimly, 'As I feared
Nothing again for me.'

'I did want crackers
And I did want candy
I know a box of chocolates

Would come in handy,
I do love oranges,
I did want nuts.
I haven't got a pocket knife —
Not one that cuts,
And, oh! if Father Christmas had loved me at all
He would have brought a big, red, india-rubber ball.'

King John stood by the window
And frowned to see below
The happy bands of boys and girls
All playing in the snow.
A while he stood there watching
And envying them all,
When through the window big and red,
There hurtled by his royal head
And bounced and fell upon the bed,
An india-rubber ball.
AND OH! FATHER CHRISTMAS
    MY BLESSINGS ON YOU FALL
FOR BRINGING HIM A BIG RED
    INDIA-RUBBER BALL!

From Abigail and Jonathan of Finchley:

How are you at the North Poal? Is it very cold? Me and my little brother Jonathan want to say happy Christmas to you. We know you work very hard but we hope you will remember to visit us. My brother would like a new slime beecos Mummy took it when the cat was sick.

From Paula Formby of London SW3:

Please may I have a liquidiser, some cheekyboo clothes, radio, motor car, reading books . . .

From Abby Mangold of London W4:

Please may I have a dolly for Christmas, Mummy will talk to you about the one I like so much.

From Anne Louise Johnson of West Wickham, Kent, aged 10:
Dear Father Christmas,

. . . p.s. I know I am too old to write to you really but I like doing this. How old are you? I would love to know because you know how old I am.

From Guy Colebourne, aged 6:
Dear Father Christmas,

I am writing to ask you about some presents, I hope inflation hasn't affected the amount of output since what I would like for Christmas is in popular demand . . . you don't have to bring it all in the sledge since it would weigh too much.

There follows a list of 35 items including a motorbike and side car, a micronaught battlecruiser and a horror set . . . !

From Sarah Parker of Preston, Lancs:
Dear Father Christmas,

For Christmas I want a little surprise. I only want a little one because it was my birthday in November and I got a bike for my birthday and for Christmas. I hope you like my letter.

From Rachel Lowther of Gargrave, Skipton, Yorks (air letter):
Dear Father Christmas, My name is Rachel Lowther and I am $5\frac{1}{2}$ years old. I go to school in my village and my teacher's name is miss clough.

For Christmas I would like a dolls house with lights, please. I hope you and your reindeers are very well and I will leave you a glass of sherry and a mince pie.

From Angie of Northumberland:
I would like a lot of toys please. I want a pet too. I like pets. I like you father christmas.

So say all of us!

ANSWERS

A J. H. Dowd cartoon from
Punch, 1945. Mary Evans
Picture Library

"And what would you like for your stocking?"
"Easter egg."

Dear Editor – I am 8 years old. Some of my little friends say there is no Santa Claus. Papa says 'If you see it in "The Sun" it's so.' Please tell me the truth, is there a Santa Claus?

On 21 September 1897, the editor of the *New York Sun* received this letter from Virginia O'Hanlon and gave what has now become the classic reply to all children who ask 'Is there really a Santa Claus?'

Virginia [the editor replied], your little friends are wrong. They have been affected by the skepticism of a skeptical age. They do not believe except they see. All minds, Virginia, whether they be men's or children's are little. In this great universe of ours man is a mere insect, an ant, in his intellect, as compared with the boundless world about him, as measured by the intelligence capable of grasping the whole truth and knowledge.

Yes, Virginia, there is a Santa Claus. He exists as certainly as love and generosity and devotion exist, and you know that they abound and give to your life its highest beauty and joy. Alas! how dreary would be the world if there were no Santa Claus! It would be as dreary as if there were no Virginias. There would be no childlike faith then, no poetry, no romance to make tolerable this existence. We should have no enjoyment except in sense and sight. The eternal light with which childhood fills the world would be extinguished.

Not believe in Santa Claus! You might as well not believe in fairies! You might get your papa to hire men to watch in all the chimneys on Christmas Eve to catch Santa Claus; but even if they did not see Santa Claus coming down, what would that prove? Nobody sees Santa Claus, but that is no sign that there is no Santa Claus. The most real things in the world are those that neither children nor men can see. Did you ever see fairies dancing on the lawn? Of course not, but that's no proof that they are not there. Nobody can conceive or imagine all the wonders there are unseen and unseeable in the world.

You tear apart the baby's rattle and see what makes the noise inside, but there is a veil covering the unseen world which not the strongest man, nor even the united strength of all the strongest men that ever lived, could tear apart. Only faith, fancy, poetry, love, romance, can push aside that curtain and view and picture the supernatural beauty and glory beyond. It is real? Ah, Virginia, in all this world there is nothing else real and abiding.

No Santa Claus! Thank God! he lives forever. A thousand years from now, Virginia, nay, ten times ten thousand years from now, he will continue to make glad the heart of childhood.